Craven Family History

Craven Family History

Gail Craven Fail

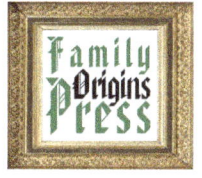

Copyright © Gail Craven Fail 2014
All Rights Reserved

ISBN: 978-0-9888632-3-1
Library of Congress Control Number:
2014952712

Family Origins Press
Dallas, Texas

For my family
Past, Present, Future

Craven Family History

I am the youngest child of Gorman Andrew Craven and Charlotte Rosebell Carlson. I was born in 1949, and I am writing this in 2014; I will be sixty-five years old soon.

My three siblings and I have become more interested in family history as we all approach the ends of our lives. I decided to put together what could be found in written documents as well as relating a few of the stories that we remember. More stories about the family are published in my brothers' books, and in my own. I have included a list of our books (at the end) as well as the sources I used to research this document. I have not referenced every fact in the paper itself. This is not intended to be a truly scholarly book.

After the reference list is a table with name, birth and death dates, and other information on each Craven man in my direct line. I am absolutely positive of the family lineage only as far back as colonial times, eight generations ago to Peter Craven the Regulator (born 1712). However, it is probable that we go back fourteen generations to an Englishman named Sir John Craven (born 1485). John's ancestors (who called themselves "de Daiville") came to England from France 400 years (about 20 generations) before Sir John's time.

I have researched Cravens only through the male line. This is not because I am ignorant of the importance of women, but because tracing every wife and her ancestry seemed impossible. Also, in very old records, a man's wife and daughters have not always been named.

My cousin Stella's daughter-in-law (Peggy Wilson) has done a huge amount of helpful research and has her information posted on Ancestry.com. She has also posted all the Craven family members gravesites in one spot, on FindAGrave.com. She has a family tree posted on Ancestry.com, called the Wilson/Short tree. Peggy's Craven tree goes back seven generations to Thomas Craven (Peter Craven's son).

I have been less concerned with absolute accuracy of birth/death/marriage dates than with the stories and the issues faced by people at various points in history. I wanted to view the Cravens within the context of their own times. I have included some information about related Cravens who were not in my direct line, but were interesting anyway.

My father Gorman told me that Craven men did not live long lives. He was referring to his immediate forebears, since he knew nothing about the more remote ones. His two uncles died fairly young, as did his father and grandfather. Mostly, Craven men have died of heart disease. Papa, whose heart condition was diagnosed when he was pretty young, was convinced he would not live long to be old. As a result, he made no provisions or plans for his own eventual retirement. He was very surprised to live into his early 70s.

In the fourteen generations before me, only eleven of the Craven men lived past the age of sixty. This is not really too bad, given the short average life expectancy of people in the past. But oddly, the longest-lived Cravens in my line were those born in the 1400s and 1500s. Sir John, his son, and his grandson lived past their nineties. My grandfather and the four generations before him lived only into their middle sixties, except for my great-great grandfather, who died at age thirty-eight.

Some Cravens had large families, and several had more than one spouse. Of course, a lot of their children died young. But starting with Peter the Regulator, who lived in colonial times, more children survived and families got very large. Peter had seven kids who lived to adulthood, the largest number in my direct line until his generation. After Peter the family sizes of Cravens in my line ranged from eight to sixteen children, until my grandparents, who had only three. There was a reason for this smaller number, which I will explain later.

Colonial families in the 1600s and 1700s were in general bigger than families in Europe. There are a number of reasons for this phenomenon, which was noticed by Benjamin Franklin. He hypothesized that in Europe, less land was available and people married later in life, so their families were smaller. Later demographers showed that he was correct. But in addition, infant mortality was lower, and food crises were less common in colonial America than in Europe. Epidemics of infectious diseases occurred in both Europe and America, but well fed people survive infections better. American colonists simply had a better standard of living than the majority of people in Europe.

Most of the Cravens in my direct line were farmers; my father and his brothers were the first generation that did not farm. Many of the Cravens were religious, and there seems to have been an unusually large number of ministers/preachers among them. Most were ordinary people, neither rich nor famous. Cravens in my line were not well educated until my generation, but they were mostly smart, hardworking people. As far as I know, there were not very many criminals among them.

The first Cravens in America came in colonial times and their descendants gradually moved westward as the nation expanded that direction. Craven history is a microcosm of English and American history.

According to Papa's family lore, three Cravens brothers came to America from England before the Revolutionary War. One remained in Pennsylvania and married a freed slave. The two others moved elsewhere. One of these two founded our Craven line. Papa said that our name originally had an "s" at the end, but the brother who was our ancestor dropped it because he did not want to have the same last name as his African American nieces and nephews.

In the mid 90s in California, I met a black man named Cravens who looked remarkably like my father, except darker. He had Papa's pointy nose, widow's peak hair pattern, stocky build and greenish eyes. His family history included the same story: three English brothers came to Pennsylvania, one married a black woman, and founded his Cravens family there. The others moved away. Both of us got some entertainment from the possibility of having common ancestors, and we called each other "cousin."

Realistically, the physical similarity between this man and my father was probably an accident. Old photos of Craven family members show no evidence of common characteristics like a pointy nose. In fact, our relatives and ancestors have had all different kinds of facial features, body types and hairlines. I was sorry to discover this, but it makes perfect sense biologically.

Papa's earliest well-documented ancestor (Peter Craven, the Regulator) lived in North Carolina in the 1700s. I found excellent information about Peter the Regulator and his descendants in two published genealogies of the Craven family, both compiled by Mary Craven Purvis. The first is *Descendants of Peter Craven, Randolph County North Carolina*, published in 1985. Her second book, *280 Years with Peter Craven Family*, came out ten years later. It is a collection of stories from many Craven family members. These books refer to Peter Craven as the Patriarch.

Through a lucky accident I was able to buy both books, which are out of print. I have used the Purvis books, material at online genealogy sites, various historical accounts, and my family's memories to describe the lives and times of the Cravens. In the second Purvis book, a Craven tells the "Three Brothers Story," which apparently was told in other Craven households also. She said that one brother stayed in Pennsylvania, one went west, and the third moved to North Carolina. Another source in the same book (but written by a different descendant) gives essentially the same story. I am positive that we are descended from Peter Craven in North Carolina. I am not sure about the three brothers story, but there might be some truth to it.

One of the problems with this search has been the irritating custom of repeating men's first names within the family. The Cravens have unimaginatively used and re-used a few common names: Robert, Thomas, John, William, Peter, and Andrew. For example, my brother Carl, cousin Andy, father, grandfather, and great grandfather were all given Andrew as a first or middle name. Looking at old records, it has been very easy to confuse cousins, since in one generation there might be several with the same name, and with birthdates the same year. While reading copies of old records I found myself longing to see a Clarence, Zephaniel, or Stanton. To be sure, I saw some interesting ones: Enoch Spinks Craven, Luther Cornelius Craven, and Isaac Newton Craven, but none of these people were in my direct line.

Craven has been spelled many different ways: Cravin, Cravens, Cravine, Craevin, Cravene, Cravant, etc. Papa never told me (and likely did not know) where the name originated. I had a vague idea it might have been Irish. There are some Irish Cravens, whose name was once Crabhan, meaning "crow." However, our family name is derived from a region in the English county of North Yorkshire. The term Craven has been used for that area since at least the 11th century.

Historians differ on what the English Craven means. It could be based on similar sounding Irish, pre-Celtic, Old English, Latin, French, Norwegian, or Welsh words, and it could have been originally a noun, verb or adverb. Besides the Irish word for crow, it might mean garlic, stony place, demand, break, strike down, or defeat. Whatever the original meaning of Craven, it had nothing to do with the more modern meaning "chicken-livered and spineless." The latter meaning was not used until the 14th century, and was probably a reference to the meaning "defeat," which came to mean "a feeling of being defeated," or "admitting defeat."

North Yorkshire showing Craven District

The district of Craven includes part of Bowland Fells, which is today considered one of the most scenic places in England. It encompasses hills, forests, bogs and peat moors, and is the remnant of a once enormous forest that was cut down by Bronze Age people. Much of Craven is land that cannot be easily cultivated. The soil is clay and hard to plow. In parts it is boggy. Higher slopes are covered with rocks. It is good sheep country. In fact, the ancient forest may have been largely cut or burned to make grazing land for sheep. But people were able to grow oats, peas, wheat and barley in some areas.

Countryside in Craven District

Craven district, like the rest of the British Isles, suffered from periodic invasions, occupations, rebellions, epidemics, and other disasters. We know something about the historic boundaries of Craven because of William the Conqueror, also called William the Bastard. In 1066 he and his army (including a Craven ancestor) arrived from Normandy (France) and took the throne of England. William's French-speaking knights were given English land stolen from the previous owners, whose ancestors had stolen it from somebody else. William's gifts of Yorkshire land came with the understanding that his knights would protect Northern England from invasions by Danes or Scots. The Normans built dozens of castles, monasteries, parish churches, and cathedrals. French became the language spoken by the court and upper classes.

After William made himself king, there were a number of rebellions in northern England. By 1071 these were completely quashed. William used a scorched earth policy, which left many people to die of starvation.

Twenty years after he took over England, the Bastard was pretty well established, but he had serious money problems. He maintained a huge army because of threats from Scandinavia, potential rebellions in England, and continual battles in mainland Europe. Tax evasion was a common problem at the time, and smart farmers would hide assets like pigs, wool, cattle, horses, and productive land from the taxmen. He commissioned an official survey of England, so that he could more efficiently collect taxes on his subjects. Because of this survey, we know the general extent of the ancient area called Craven.

The book containing William the Bastard's survey data was commonly called the Domesday Book (meaning Day of Judgment) because there was no appealing its data regarding land or material wealth. It includes records of villages, names of landowners, tenants, slaves, areas of woodland, meadows, animals, ponds and plowed land. Almost all of the villages listed in the Domesday Book as being part of Craven are still in existence. The 11th century Craven covered a much larger area than the modern district of Craven in northern England.

The Domesday Book

William the Conqueror

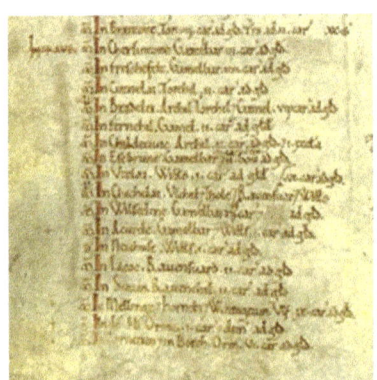

Domesday Book list of arable land in Craven District

According to *The Norman People and Their Existing Descendants in the British Dominions and the United States of America,* the Cravens came from a Norman family, the de Daivilles (also spelled Deville, Devil, Davell, Dayvill, etc.). Walter de Daiville came to England with William the Conqueror in 1066, and was rewarded for his service with property in York. His name may have meant "from the Devil," which was once a common name for a young man who got in trouble. But more likely it meant he was from the ancient Norman village of Deville, in northeastern France. The modern village is a popular tourist spot.

Deville, France

The de Daivilles' Yorkshire land was passed along through several generations of de Daivilles. Eventually, a Robert de Daiville married a woman whose dowry included some property in the district of Craven. By 1316, one of his descendants was calling himself William de Craven. He was the ancestor of the Cravens of Appletreewick, from whom we are probably descended.

The earliest person I found to use the last name Craven was Robert de Craven, who was born in the late 1200s at the beginning of the Late Middle Ages. This was almost two hundred years after William the Bastard invaded. I am not sure whether Robert was a relative, but several other Ancestry.com family trees list him as an ancestor of Peter Craven, so I felt obliged to include him, too.

Robert de Craven was rector for the Church of Saint Peter and Saint Paul, in a little village named Bolton by Bowland, in the region of Craven. Church records show he was rector starting in 1304. His church was very close to the Appletreewick Cravens from whom we are probably descended.

A rector was a parish priest who was paid directly by tithes from his parishioners. In some cases, a rector was absent from the parish, and his duties were given to a substitute, who did the work for a smaller portion of the tithes. The old church record does not indicate whether Robert de Craven was actually the resident priest or whether he subcontracted his priestly duties to someone else.

A rectorship was a desirable appointment, especially in a reasonably well-to-do parish. It was usually a lifetime job, unless the rector screwed up in some way and angered his bishop or the local gentry. Like most of Yorkshire, Bolton by Bowland was rural and not outstandingly wealthy, but the parish included decent farm and grazing land, as well as metal mines. Robert would have had a relatively comfortable life, compared to most of his parishioners. As a priest, he must have had some education. At the time, the literacy rate among the general population was only about 1%.

Robert may or may not have been celibate. There is a disagreement among Catholic historians regarding exactly when celibacy became mandatory for priests. In the early 1100s Pope Innocent II decreed that all priestly marriages were annulled. This was a move to protect Church property and membership in the priesthood from being handed down from father to son. But by the 14th century, some priests were still marrying, and even Popes continued to have mistresses, wives, and children.

Anglican Church of Saint Peter and Saint Paul

Robert's Catholic Church of Saint Peter and Saint Paul was built in about 1190, so when Robert was rector the church was already more than a century old. The Anglican Church currently at that site (and with the same name) has been rebuilt several times, so nothing remains of the original structure. The Anglican Church records include some of those from the original Catholic Church. Their list of rectors actually begins with Robert de Craven, who was invested in 1304. He was rector for two years, and then replaced, but the record does not say why. Records of subsequent rectors are more complete, and show that they mainly vacated their positions by dying. Average life expectancy in the early 1300s was only 30 years, so a lifetime appointment might not have been very long.

Robert may have been related to the Cravens from whom I am descended. I assume others in his family named themselves "de Craven" as well, but any number of unrelated people from that area could have taken the same name.

Between the 11th and 13th centuries, a time called the High Middle Ages, Europe was reasonably prosperous, in spite of the usual arguments over who should be King, disagreements with the Pope, a major split of the Catholic Church into Eastern and Western branches, persecution of Jews and heretics, crusades against Muslims, and numerous wars in Europe. The climate was relatively warm, and rains fell at the appropriate times to support crops. As a result, the population grew.

By the early 1300s, England's population had expanded past its ability to feed itself. Along with over-farming and soil depletion, there were several years of cold, wet weather, resulting in the Great Famine of 1315-1317. The weather changes were caused by the five-year long eruption of a large volcano in New Zealand, which lowered average temperatures worldwide. The Craven family would most certainly have been affected by the famine, which led to millions of deaths from starvation. Between 10% and 25% of the English population died in the Great Famine.

In 1327 the Black Death (bubonic plague) hit an already weakened England and at the same time, the nation went to war with France. The war (called later the Hundred Year War) drained England of young men and other resources. But the plague, which hit Yorkshire and the Craven district in 1349, eventually killed almost half of England.

The consequences of these fourteenth century disasters, especially the plague, were profound. The Catholic Church was the only legally sanctioned church, but God did not answer the prayers of good Catholics during the Great Famine and Black Death years. Some people blamed a corrupt Church for the displeasure of God, laying a foundation for later movements against the Church. The loss of workers for farming, carpentry, and other essential jobs changed the feudal system. Workers were in such short supply that wealthier people had to pay more for their work. This helped establish a middle class. The plague also led to more persecutions of Jews, foreigners, and others who could be blamed for the disease.

Our ancestors (at least some of them) survived all these terrible events and in 1485, a man named John Craven (a descendant of the de Daivilles) was born in Appletreewick, a village in the Craven district about 25 miles west of Robert de Craven's church.

John's parents lived during the time of the Wars of the Roses (mid 1450s to late 1480s), a long conflict between two royal families, the Houses of Lancaster (symbolized by a red rose) and York (white rose). The conflict was the result of the Hundred Years War (which created terrible social and financial difficulties) and a relatively weak and possibly lunatic king, Henry VI. The wars ended with the defeat of the Yorkists and the coronation of Lancastrian Henry Tudor, who then married a York woman and united the two houses. The Wars split the nobility into factions, and many of them died in battle.

A biography of Elizabeth Stuart, daughter of King James I, states that the Cravens had become impoverished during the "feuds of the two roses," indicating they supported the wrong king. Most of the land-owning families in the Craven district were Yorkists, and much of the actual fighting occurred in North Yorkshire. The Cravens were not alone in the loss of their fortunes during that period.

Modern Appletreewick (pronounced "Aptrick" by locals) has a population of about 200 people. It is a popular tourist destination, with picturesque ancient stone houses, steep streets, and an ivy-covered pub named the Craven Arms, established by John Craven's grandson. I am especially happy to claim a pub as part of the family history. John and some of his children and grandchildren stayed in the Craven district, where they owned property. Some of his descendants still live there.

Craven Arms Pub

Appletreewick street

John Craven lived to be 100 years old, a remarkable age even for modern times. His lifespan encompassed the rule of the Tudors. He was born the same year Henry VII became King, and saw the reigns of Henry VIII, Edward VI, Jane Grey, Mary I and Elizabeth I. He must have had an excellent immune system and the advantage of enough to eat. John had only one surviving child, William.

Henry VIII separated the English Catholic

Church (Anglican Church) from the Roman Catholic Church in the 1530s. He insisted that the Bible be translated into English, so everyone could understand what was read in church. During the sixteenth and seventeenth centuries there were a number of dissident groups who separated from the Anglican Church. Most of these groups no longer exist. But the Baptists, Presbyterians, Quakers, and Unitarians survived. The Methodist Church came out of the Anglican Church later, in the eighteenth century.

Catholicism in England was almost completely destroyed by Henry VIII, who tore down many Catholic churches, abbeys, and nunneries and confiscated their wealth. I am not sure about the religious convictions of John Craven and his children, but I assume they wisely became Anglicans or kept a fairly low profile, especially after having supported the losers in the Wars of the Roses during the previous generation.

John is called "Sir John" in old records, but I don't know when or why he was knighted. However, being a knight at that time did not necessarily mean that he was a professional soldier, or that he had any significant wealth. In fact, historians say that John Craven's family was poor until his grandson (William II) got rich from selling wool and silk.

Sir John and his descendants are listed in Burke's Dictionary of the Landed Gentry of Great Britain and Ireland, so they were landowners. Sir John and his sons for four generations were knights. His ancestor, Walter de Daiville, was also a knight. I don't know anything about the de Daiville/Craven men in the four hundred years between them. Written records were few during that time.

By the time Sir John was born, knighthood was an established way of honoring men for military service, bravery, or just doing a large favor for the monarch. But many knights of the time were not armored men riding warhorses into battle. Some were landowners and farmers, although their tenants did the actual labor of working the land.

John's son, Sir William Craven I, was born around 1503, in the village of Appletreewick. As an adult, he lived in a small cottage in the nearby village of Burnsall. William (who lived to age 96) and his wife Beatrix had three sons: Anthony (from whom I am probably descended), Henry, and William II. The boys were educated at a Dames School in Burnsall. This was a place for children of poor working families to get a basic education before they went to work.

Of William's three sons, William II is the most famous. He became the Lord Mayor of London, and was the Craven who built the pub in Appletreewick. I have included more information about William II and his son William III than about my ancestor Anthony, simply because the Williams were so famous and interesting, and it was William II and William III who brought the family to prominence and wealth. Anthony seems to have stayed quietly at home in Craven District, farmed and raised his children. Not much is known about him.

One historian (W. J. Stavert) claims that the lineage I have described so far is wrong. He published a short article entitled "Notes on the Pedigree of the Cravens of Appletreewick" in the Yorkshire Archeological Journal in 1895. Stavert says that all other

Craven historians were wrong and they mistook Sir Anthony, the son of William I and Beatrix, with a different Anthony Craven, who was actually a cousin of William I. This complicates the picture so much that I have decided that Stavert was a nutcase whose material should be ignored. However, I am not positive about that. It is another instance of confusion wrought by repetition of first names by Cravens of that era.

The village of Burnsall, where William I's sons were born, has a modern population of just over a hundred people. It was likely not any bigger in the 1500s. William's son, William II, built a grammar school in Burnsall in 1602. Amazingly, that handsome and historic building is still in use as a school. I assume they have upgraded the sanitary facilities. Besides building a grammar school in Burnsall, William II also rebuilt the church in Burnsall, and bought and refurbished the manor house in Burnsall, right across the street from the modest cottage where he was born. It seems a way of thumbing his nose at the local gentry, who may have looked down on the poor Cravens.

Old Grammar School in Burnsall, founded by William Craven II in 1611

William II left the Craven district in his early teens and was apprenticed to a fabric merchant. He did phenomenally well selling wool and silk, and by his forties (during the reign of Queen Elizabeth) he was living in a mansion in London. He spent a fair amount of money in his home district, improving conditions for the local people and his relatives. His son continued this habit, making the Appletreewick and Burnsall Cravens much more prosperous. William II left his brothers and their children sizeable bequests in his will. His fortune was worth the equivalent of five billion pounds, in modern money. This made him one of the ten richest men in England at the time of his death.

Sir William II

As William II got richer his political influence increased. In his early fifties he became the Sheriff of London, an elected position drawn from the combined guilds of the time, which were called Livery Companies. The 106 livery companies in London included William's company, the drapers (cloth merchants), as well as basketmakers, coopers, grocers, tobacco blenders, tax advisors, distillers and others. These guilds had a significant amount of political power because they controlled a great deal of the nation's wealth.

A few years after Queen Elizabeth died, William II became the Lord Mayor of London, another elected position. He was well liked at court, possibly because he was in a position to loan money to the King, James I, who knighted William. The knighthood came when William was 55 years old.

At age 57, William II married the young daughter of a wealthy guild member. He and his wife rubbed shoulders with royalty, made charitable donations, and sent poorer Craven relatives to University. They had five children, and he died at age 70. His children married well, except for one son, William III. This son became a soldier and never married. His life story is fascinating and somewhat romantic. He was educated at Oxford, entered military service at age sixteen, and was knighted at twenty-one.

Sir William III, in his curly wig

The third William took the King's side in the English Civil War (1642-1651) when the supporters of King Charles I and the "Roundheads" or Parliamentarians fought over the nature of British government, religion, and the authority of the King. He was not actually in England during the Civil War, because he had taken service with King Charles' sister Elizabeth Stuart and her husband Frederick V, King of Bohemia.

Apparently during this time William III fell in love with Elizabeth, who was about twelve years older than he. There is no indication that their love was anything but platonic. William gave financial support to Elizabeth's brother, King Charles I, until the Roundheads chopped off Charles' head. The new government confiscated some of William III's English lands and wealth as a result of his support for the King. However, he was still rich.

The Roundheads were named because they did not wear the elaborate curled wigs worn by courtly men. Many of the Roundheads were Puritans or Presbyterians, although some were Anglicans. The famous Oliver Cromwell, a Roundhead Puritan, took control of the country until 1658. When he died, the power vacuum was so severe that the monarchy was restored and Charles II was invited back to England in 1660.

When Charles II returned to England (he had been hiding out in Europe to avoid getting his own head chopped off) William Craven III came along. By that time he was a trusted friend and confidant of the Stuart family, and the new king rewarded his loyalty. William got back his property, was made a peer (1st Earl of Craven) and was given a share in the Colony of Carolina. Craven County, North Carolina, is named after William Craven III.

During the English Civil War, Elizabeth and her husband Frederick lost their Bohemian monarchy in some of the constant European unrest of the time, and lived in exile in Holland. After her nephew Charles II was restored to the throne, Elizabeth (now a widow) asked that she and her many children be allowed to return to England. She was penniless, and had been supported entirely by William Craven while in exile. Charles II refused to fund her return, or to support her once she had safely returned to England. Maybe she had so many children that Charles did not want the cost of caring for the lot. Instead, William paid for her return. She and her children lived with him. It was a fairly scandalous relationship, and some historians have suggested that they were secretly married. At the very least, it was an unusual event for an upper class unmarried lady to live with a gentleman. She lived with him until her death, and left him all her family portraits and personal records.

William III was well known for his military prowess, courage, and his blunt and often obscene language. His lack of pretty social skills led to being scorned by some of Elizabeth's children, who nonetheless accepted his money. But he was a proud man. William famously said to the Earl of Oxford, who could trace his ancestry back several hundred years, "I am William Lord Craven; my father was Lord Mayor of London, and my grandfather was the Lord knows who; wherefore I think my pedigree as good as yours, my lord." My father Gorman would have liked William's sentiment. He had little patience with people who gave themselves airs because of their ancestors being wealthy or famous.

Several publications were dedicated to William III, who was generous with money to support writers and artists. A book of poems written by John Donne and published posthumously by his son is dedicated to "The Right Honorable William Lord Craven." There is a wordy preface to this book, praising Lord Craven's generosity. It ends by stating: "that in your lordship we may still read a most perfect character of what England was in all her pomp and greatness, so that although these poems were formerly written upon several occasions, and to several persons, they now unite themselves, and are become one pyramid to set your lordship's statue upon, where you may stand like armed Apollo the defender of the Muses, encouraging the poets now alive to celebrate your great acts by affording your countenance to his poems that wanted only so noble a subject."

This over-blown praise made me laugh out loud, and may have done the same for Lord Craven.

William III, along with other wealthy men and members of the royal family, made money in African slave trading after the Restoration. He was renowned for helping Londoners during an outbreak of the plague, and for helping fight the great fire of London in 1666. It was said that his horse was trained to run toward the smell of burning, rather than away. Perhaps his best-known quality was his life-long devotion to Elizabeth Stuart. William III died unmarried at age 88. His love for Elizabeth Stuart has been the subject of several historical romances. One writer claims that the enormous house he planned and built for Elizabeth (but which she never occupied, dying before completion) was made in the shape of a phallus, a testament to their sexual relationship.

Sir Anthony Craven, my putative ancestor, was the oldest son of Sir William I, and William II's brother. Like his father, he lived to a very old age, dying at 95. Anthony waited until he was 35 to get married, and then took a 12 year-old girl, Anne Crofte, as wife. Anne had the first of six children a year later. Anne's tender age at marriage was not too unusual in the 1500s, at least in wealthier families. It was legal then for girls to marry at 12, boys at 14, with parental permission.

William II probably arranged Anthony's match, since by the time they married William was already wealthy and influential. I am not sure how Anthony came to be knighted, but it may have been his brother's position leading to that honor.

Anthony and Anne lived in Darley, about 10 miles from Appletreewick. The modern village of Darley has about 1200 people and is locally well known for its gardens. It has been voted the Best Large Village in Yorkshire several times. It is interesting that 1200 people make it a Large Village.

Area near Darley, Yorkshire

Anthony's son Thomas, born in 1585, married his first cousin Margaret Craven. I have very little information about Thomas and Margaret. Their children included Sir Robert Craven, whose widow Anne and children moved to the American Colonies after

Robert's death.

Anne Craven's story is an interesting one. Her husband, Sir Robert Craven, was given a job by his cousin, Lord Craven, William III. Robert was "Master of the Horse" for Elizabeth Stuart after she returned from exile in Holland. This position was considered an huge honor. Since Elizabeth had no money and was entirely dependent on William III, the horses actually belonged to William. But the honor of being the Master of Horse for the Queen of Bohemia was so significant that it is written on Robert's tombstone.

Robert Craven was educated at Oxford, at his cousin's expense. While there, he became a friend of George Fox, the founder of the Quaker movement (Society of Friends) and a strong proponent of the novel idea that women had souls. Both Robert and his wife Ann were Quakers. They married in a Quaker church, the Middlesex County Friends Church in 1667. By the time they married, Quakers had already suffered from severe persecution in England. The English parliament passed the Act of Uniformity in 1662, proscribing the particular form of worship practiced by Quakers. George Fox spent some time in jail. Professing a faith in Quaker principles required a great deal of courage. Fox lists Robert Craven as one of the Friends who supported him in the 1650s. In this writing, Robert is said to have been one of the previous Sheriffs of Lincoln. I am not sure whether this is the same Robert Craven as my ancestor.

The Quakers referred to themselves as "Friends." The term Quaker was applied because George Fox told people to "tremble at the word of the Lord." The term was at first a derogatory one, but became widely accepted, even by the Friends themselves. Quakers were not Puritans, although George Fox was born and raised in a strongly Puritan town in England. In fact, Quakers disagreed with many of the Puritan ideas, particularly that of predestination, the idea that God has already chosen who will be sent to heaven and who will be eternally damned. I have a problem with that idea, myself.

Robert drowned at age 40, about ten years after Elizabeth Stuart's death. In 1676, a few years after Robert died, Anne moved to the colonies with her children Thomas, Ann and Peter. There may have been a third son also, which would explain the three brothers story in family lore. But the colonial records I have seen online do not mention a third son.

I am not certain what William III thought of his relative's Quakerism. William lived about twenty years past the time that Robert's wife moved to America.

Anne settled in John Fenwick's Quaker Colony in Salem, New Jersey. Fenwick, the son of a wealthy and influential family, acquired title to a large tract of land on the Delaware River and brought over the first shipload of Quakers only two years before Ann immigrated. A few previous Europeans, including English, Swedes, Dutch, and Finns, had already settled the area, and had developed mostly peaceful relations with the native people. To assure continued good relations, Fenwick "bought" the land from the natives with guns, gunpowder and rum. This strikes me as most un-Quakerish, but maybe not too surprising, since Fenwick had been a soldier before he became a Quaker.

A famous oak tree in Salem marks the spot

where Fenwick supposedly made his treaty with the Indians.

The Treaty Oak commemorating John Fenwick

Fenwick's Quaker colony was well enough established by 1676 that Anne must have felt confident of being safe and among people she trusted. Several shiploads of Quakers came to Salem in the mid to late 1670s, and Anne sailed on one of these. Quaker families took along their livestock and household goods, including all the nails and tools needed to build their houses. Considering that the sailing time was a bit over two months and Anne had three small children under the age of eight, it must have been a somewhat uncomfortable voyage. I think she was very brave.

The Colonies

Anne purchased 300 acres of land near the Delaware River and called the property "Craven's

Choyce." The land was described as "fast land marsh and swamp." (Fast land is property that is not permanently flooded, but is near water.) Anne probably farmed the land, or rented it to someone else to farm. Settlers at that time were able to produce good crops of flax, hemp, wheat and vegetables. They also cut and exported timber.

Fast land and swamp near the Delaware River in New Jersey

Three years after she bought the land, Anne married a tanner named Edward Bagley, who outlived her. When Anne died in her mid fifties, Quaker neighbors took the children. Bagley remarried after Anne's death, and there was apparently some friction between him and his stepchildren.

The story of what happened to Anne and Robert's children is fuzzy. There are colonial records of a man named Joshua Peter Craven, born in 1671 in England. The birth date fits Anne and Robert's son Peter. Some sources claim that Anne's son Peter died without children, others that he had children with an Indian woman. The two books by Mary Craven Purvis indicate that we are descended from Joshua Peter. I assume Joshua Peter Craven was actually Ann's son and that he was my ancestor.

We know that Joshua Peter Craven was born in England and immigrated to New Jersey's Quaker colony, which matches the experience of Anne's son Peter. He married a woman from Virginia and had three sons, one of whom was Peter Craven. There isn't much else known about Joshua Peter. But the birth (1712), death (1794), descendants and life events of his son Peter Craven (also referred to as Peter the Regulator, Peter the Potter, or Peter the Patriarch) are well documented in early American records, and this second Peter was definitely my ancestor.

Over about 250 years, descendants of Peter the Regulator in my line moved from New Jersey to Virginia, North Carolina, Mississippi, Arkansas, Oklahoma, and finally to Texas, where most of my generation was born. Like many colonial families, there was a gradual movement west, as each successive generation looked for new, more fertile farmland and the older territories filled up with people.

Peter Craven, the Regulator, was born in the Quaker colony of Salem County, New Jersey. He was a farmer, as most colonial people were at that time, but he was also a potter. America had all the raw material for potting: clay was abundant, and there were plenty of trees for firing kilns. The limiting factor for pottery products in colonial times was the skill required to make good pottery. I am not sure how Peter learned the trade, but he did not depend solely on potting for a livelihood. He was primarily a farmer.

None of Peter's pottery has survived to modern times, but he taught his children, and was the first of several generations of potters. Lin Craven, one of his descendants (not in my direct line) is a famous Georgia potter whose work is shown at the Smithsonian. Reverend John Craven, Peter's grandson, is given credit for founding the well-known Craven potters in North Carolina.

Potters in colonial times made simple utilitarian objects like jugs for holding whiskey, cane syrup, or cider and common household items such as butter churns and chamber pots. The British laws at the time prohibited colonial potters from making and selling fancy porcelain pieces because they wanted no competition for the English manufacturers. Since metal and glass containers were unavailable, pottery was used for almost everything.

Peter Craven and his wife (whose name is unknown) had six sons and at least one daughter. Peter moved his family several times to avoid paying taxes. This aversion to taxes was every bit as strong in my father, so it might be a family trait that was passed along. By 1744, the same year his second son was born, Peter and his wife had left New Jersey for Augusta County, Virginia. A year later they moved with five other Quaker families to North Carolina. The group traveled along the Great Wagon Road, which had once been a Native American foot trail. This road was the main route used by migrants moving into the southern coastal regions, and it ran from Philadelphia to South Carolina. Quakers were among the first Christians to settle in North Carolina.

They settled in the Piedmont region, a beautiful area of gently rolling hills and forests that forms the foothills of the Appalachians. The red clay soil there was fertile, and farmers could grow healthy crops of tobacco, corn, and vegetables. The Cravens got a grant for almost 600 acres of land in what is now Randolph County. The family prospered. By the late 1700s, much of the land around Peter's property was owned by Peter's offspring. The area they settled was south of Ramseur and near Coleridge, North Carolina.

The Piedmont

Peter found an ideal location. His land had a natural spring, and there was a river nearby (Deep River). A small stream called Back Branch crossed the land. Local clay deposits made attractive earthenware pottery in colors of yellow, pumpkin, and rust. Wild game and fish were abundant. A road crossed his land, making travel more convenient, and the Cravens were only thirty miles (about 2 days ride) from the colonial town of Hillsborough, with the nearest courthouse. The road eventually became the first mail route in eastern Randolph County. Peter's property adjoined what is now the Concord Methodist Church Cemetery, where Peter and many of his descendants are buried.

Peter and his family cut timber and built a house in two sections, connected by a breezeway between. This style is called a dogtrot house. There were many built in the Southeastern U.S, in the 19th century, and historians believe the dogtrot style originated in the Piedmont region of the Carolinas. The dogtrot, or breezeway, between the two sections of the house formed a cooler covered area for sitting. It was a place where, on hot summer days, people could sew, snap beans, spin, whittle, and do other jobs while sitting.

A Dogtrot House in Georgia

The chimneys of Peter's home were constructed from local stone, logs were chinked with local clay, and foundations were formed of hand made brick. He built his pottery shop right next to the spring. He built it well, because this building was used for making pots over the next four generations. He also built a barn, granary, and smokehouse. Peter's home-site is still owned by a Craven descendant. The home itself is gone, but the original cornerstones and foundations are still in place, and the current Cravens continue to turn up old handmade bricks and pottery shards in the vicinity. The area near the spring was used for a muster ground during the Civil War, and later was a voting and public speaking site.

In the 1740s, about when Peter left New Jersey, there was a Protestant Christian movement called the Great Awakening sweeping across Great Britain and the Colonies. This movement had a big impact on religion in America. There was a de-emphasis on ceremony and ritual, along with an increased personal relationship with God. Itinerant preachers (many with no formal education) carried the message into the colonial backwoods. Peter's children and grandchildren, like many other North Carolinians, were strongly influenced by the Great Awakening.

Peter did not keep to the strict non-violence that Quakers espoused, and he probably associated with one of the other Protestant churches in his area. When he was in his early 50s and well established in his local North Carolina community, he joined a group of farmer/protestors who called themselves the Regulators. These men were fed up with crooked colonial officials. Regulator activities lasted for about 5 years, starting in 1764. Several thousand people were either directly involved with or sympathetic to the Regulators. The Regulator movement in North and South

Carolina was one of the first rumblings leading to the Revolutionary War.

The Regulators were not actually rebelling against the English Crown, but were fighting unscrupulous officials and the system that allowed them to flourish. They tried to get North Carolina's colonial governor, William Tryon, to change things. When this was unsuccessful, they rioted, refused to pay their taxes, and beat up several officials, including judges and attorneys. This was decidedly not Quaker-like behavior. In fact, some historians claim that except for one Quaker (who did not fight) most of the Regulators were Baptists.

North Carolina's openly corrupt officials demanded bribes, double-taxed many people, charged outrageous sums for marriage licenses and court costs, and confiscated essential things like plow horses to satisfy debts. A sheriff could show up unannounced at a farmer's home, demand immediate payment of taxes in cash, and then confiscate the land if the taxes were not paid. The land would be sold cheaply to cronies of the sheriff. One farmer's wife was stripped nude and her homespun dress sold at auction.

In 1767, after several attempts at making reasonably polite demands, the Regulators met at Sandy Creek, N.C., and wrote another document. They stated that they would refuse to pay taxes until they got redress. Peter Craven was chosen as their representative to confer with county officials regarding this latest document. When Peter rode into Hillsborough, the county seat, the sheriff immediately seized his horse for nonpayment of taxes. This act inflamed people so much that an armed mob of Regulators, including Peter and his two oldest sons, came to the county seat, stole the horse back, rioted, tied up the sheriff, dragged him and his deputies through town, and fired shots into houses.

The governor reacted to the violence by raising the militia and ordering the arrest of several of the Regulators, including Peter. They were jailed in Hillsborough. At the same time, Governor Tryon had Edward Fanning, one of his more outrageously crooked subordinates, arrested for extortion.

Peter and the other Regulators jailed with him were tried, found guilty, fined fifty pounds and given a six-month sentence. The governor almost immediately pardoned them. Fanning was found guilty of extortion but was fined only one penny per count, with no jail time. This slap on the wrist further inflamed the Regulators.

Most of the militiamen conscripted by the governor came from outside the area, but some were local. Many of these locally conscripted soldiers refused to fight, taking the side of the farmers, who were, after all, their own friends and neighbors.

The Regulator movement ended after the famous Battle of Alamance, when Tryon's militia soundly defeated the Regulators in only two hours. During this battle, the poorly trained and armed Regulators faced a larger number of well-armed militia with cannons. There is a stirring description of the battle in Centennial History of Alamance County 1849 - 1949 by Walter Whitaker, published by the Burlington N. C. Chamber of Commerce in 1949. Many of the Regulators, including Peter, were active fighters later in the Revolutionary War. A less emotional description of the

Regulators can be found online in a book titled *The Roots of Appalachian Christianity*, by John Sparks, 2001.

On the day of the Battle of Alamance, Governor Tryon's redcoats and the Regulators were facing off. Tryon sent a message to the Regulators that they must surrender, but offered no guarantee of clemency or justice. One of the Regulators, Robert Thompson, was chosen to confront Governor Tryon one last time. After speaking to Tryon, he turned to leave the governor's presence, but Tryon grabbed a musket and shot Thompson in the back, killing him. He almost immediately regretted this and sent a man carrying a white truce flag to the Regulators. But the truce flag was shot from the bearer's hand. Tryon ordered his men to advance and fire. One of the Regulators famously shouted back, "Fire and be damned!"

The British militia won the battle and over the next few days, ran amok and burned farms and homes belonging to known members of the Regulators. Fortunately, Peter's home was not one of those burned. He and his family survived both the Alamance violence and the War for Independence, a few years later.

After the Battle of Alamance, Peter was one of twelve men who were arrested and taken to the Hillsborough jail. There was a trial and six were hanged. Peter and the other five were released, but I am not sure why. Two weeks later Governor Tryon offered pardons to everyone who would take an oath to King George. By that time, Tryon was tired of the entire situation and getting ready to move to another job.

The Battle of Alamance

Two other Craven men, Thomas and John, were involved in the Hillsborough riot, and fought in the Battle of Alamance. These were Peter's two older sons, who were at that time, 25 and 17 years old, respectively.

Peter and Thomas supported the War of Independence by donating supplies in 1782 and 1783, and both fought in the war. In the Purvis books, Peter's youngest son Henry is said to have been "for the King." This must have led to some family tension. However, it appears to have been resolved, because toward the end of his life, Peter lived with Henry and his wife, and Henry named his first son after his father.

From the 1760s until the middle 1780s (after the war) the Piedmont region, like much of colonial America, suffered from chaos and a lack of civil order. There were battles very near the Craven farms. It must have been an extremely difficult time for the Craven family, although we don't know the details of their experiences.

The first actual battles in the Revolution (if you discount the Battle of Alamance) were in New England in 1775. Independence was declared a year later. But it was 1780 before fighting came to Randolph County, North Carolina. That year, Charleston, SC fell to the British, and Congress sent soldiers from Delaware and Rhode Island into the area. In a classic example of poor military planning, they came without food or other supplies and so bought rations from local farmers. There are records showing Peter's payment for flour and other supplies.

Peter had seven children, but his wife's name and origin are unknown. Starting with Peter's children, records of wives and children are more complete. Some Craven descendants in North Carolina believe Peter's wife was an Indian. This is based on family stories and a drawing of one of Peter's grandsons, Rev. Jacob Craven, who supposedly looked very Indian. A copy of this portrait is in the first Purvis book, and I have my doubts. I have included it below, so you can make up your own mind.

Rev. Craven, supposedly resembling a Native American

Peter died in 1794 at age 82, and was buried in what is now the Concord Methodist Cemetery in Randolph County. The cemetery was part of Peter's original land grant, which he set aside as a graveyard.

The site of his actual grave is lost, but the cemetery has a fancy modern stone erected by some of his descendants in the 1970s. They used Olde English spelling on the marker, which makes it look more authentic.

Cemetery marker erected by Craven family members in 1978

Peter and his descendants turned away from the Quaker philosophy and joined other protestant churches. A significant number became Methodist or Baptist ministers. Strong religious belief has been a recurrent trait in the Craven family. My own grandfather and great grandfather were Baptist preachers. In 1755 a Baptist church was built in Sandy Creek, not far from Peter Craven's home. The energetic Baptists spread their gospel so efficiently that by the time of the American Revolution, they were the largest denomination in North Carolina.

Sandy Creek Baptist Church, built in 1755

The Sandy Creek community is one place where the Regulators met.

Of Peter's six sons, one (Joseph) moved to Tennessee and the rest stayed in North Carolina. The original homestead went to the oldest son Thomas, who left it to his son Solomon. It was passed along until the present generation, but along the way some of the farmland was sold, in some cases to other Cravens.

Thomas was my ancestor, and one who stayed home. He got a large grant of land near his parents. When he was 19, he married a 15-year-old girl named Frances, settled down, raised twelve children, farmed, and sold pottery. At the time of the Battle of Alamance, Thomas and Frances already had the first of their dozen offspring. Peter and his wife had young children at the same time, so some of Peter's children were not much older than his grandchildren. This was common at the time, when people married young and no birth control was available.

Thomas became a Justice of the Peace after the Revolutionary War. He died at age 74, and was buried in the same Methodist cemetery as his father. Thomas' original gravestone is still there. His will, recorded in 1814, three years before he died, left his land to his wife and several particular bequests to his children. These included 134 acres (and Peter's original home) to his son Solomon, a rifle to Jacob, ten dollars each to the daughters, and a loom to Fanny. Looms were valuable household items at the time, and not everyone could use one skillfully. Apparently Fanny was the best weaver of the family.

The next Craven in our direct line was Thomas' son John, a potter and Methodist minister. Reverend John married twice and had thirteen children. Like Thomas, he lived his entire life in North Carolina. At least two of his sons and several of his grandchildren became ministers, and some of his offspring fought in the Civil War.

In the mid 1820s, the Concord United Methodist Church in Coleridge was founded. The founding members included several Cravens. That church still exists, although it has been rebuilt and moved several times. It has old stained glass windows bearing the Craven name. At this point in our family line, most Cravens were apparently Methodists. I am not sure whether the Coleridge church is where John was a Preacher.

Concord United Methodist Church

I have found nothing in the Purvis genealogy books that shows John got any formal education in theology, so I am assuming he was a Methodist lay preacher.

The Methodist movement started in the mid 1700s, with the writings of John Wesley and his brother Charles, both Anglican priests. They were evangelicals whose teachings emphasized social service, helping the poor, and vigorous missionary activity. The movement thrived among working class people. Methodists sent both ordained and lay preachers around the globe. America had a shortage of Anglican priests after the Revolutionary War, and Methodists ordained many itinerant preachers who immigrated there in the late 1700s. The first Methodist church in North Carolina was built in 1771, about a quarter century after Peter the Regulator settled there. By 1786 the first Methodist group in Randolph County, North Carolina, was organized.

Baptists, Methodists and other Protestant churches formed as part of the Great Awakening, and resulted in the type of church services I saw as a child in evangelical churches. I imagine that a modern Protestant church service would have seemed pretty familiar to Rev. John, except for the teen-agers texting on their smart phones.

Along with religion, Reverend John passed on his knowledge of making pots. Four of his sons and several grandchildren became potters. Some of his children moved west, including my own great grandfather, Andrew Robert Craven, who had an astonishing sixteen children. Andrew Robert was also a potter, something I had not known until reading the Purvis books on Craven genealogy.

Two-gallon pottery jug made by Reverend John Craven, late 1700s

Andrew Robert married his first wife, Elizabeth, in about 1825. He was twenty-three, and his wife twenty-one. In 1840, at age thirty-eight, Andrew Robert and his family left North Carolina and moved to Mississippi. Three of his brothers had already moved to Georgia by the time Andrew left North Carolina. There were some strong incentives for their moves.

Things at home were grim. The North Carolina state legislature was not responsive to the need for education, so there were no public schools. There was no leadership for agricultural reforms. Old fashioned farming methods had depleted the soil, and state roads for getting crops to market were in bad shape. Farms that had been prosperous in the late 1700s were no longer profitable. In the early to mid 1800s, hundreds of thousands of farmers moved from North Carolina to find cheap, fertile land in Tennessee, Georgia, Indiana, Alabama, Mississippi, and Missouri. By 1860, thirty percent of the native born people of North Carolina had left.

Elizabeth died five years after the move to Mississippi, while birthing her ninth child. That child was my great-grandfather William Jasper Craven.

Within a year of Elizabeth's death, Andrew

married a teenager, Nancy Ann, with whom he had seven more children. I cannot imagine the courage it took for a young girl to marry an older widower with nine kids, knowing she would likely have many babies of her own. When Nancy Ann married Andrew, he had children ranging in age from one to seventeen (the same age as his new bride).

After his second marriage, Andrew Robert moved his family to Tennessee. A few years later they moved another 150 miles to Greene County in northeastern Arkansas, near what is now the town of Paragould. Greene County borders Missouri. I am not sure what led to each subsequent move, but assume it was the need for better farmland and the demands of supporting an ever-increasing family. Andrew lived to age 65, and was buried in the Center Hill Cemetery in Paragould. He supported himself and his family by both farming and potting.

Center Hill Cemetery, Paragould

The state of Arkansas was established in 1836. It was only twenty-one years after that date when Andrew Robert moved his family there. In the 1850s, Arkansas was still a frontier state. By 1857, when Andrew Robert arrived, the state was experiencing an economic boom, largely due to slavery-based plantation-style cotton production. This big boom was occurring in the more fertile southern lowlands of the West Gulf Coastal Plain, but Andrew's farm was in the northeast, part of the Mississippi Alluvial Plain. His land was not as fertile as the southwestern parts of the state. In Andrew's region, most farmers practiced subsistence farming on small parcels of land rather than large plantations. Few had slaves.

The region around Paragould was covered in forest, so Andrew may have had to cut trees before he could farm. Once the railroad came through Paragould, in 1872, hardwood timber was the area's main export. There were other Cravens already in Arkansas, which may have been one reason why Andrew came. One Craven family in Calhoun County (about 200 miles south of Paragould) had a son named William Jasper Craven, born in 1849. Andrew's son by the same name was born in 1845. The similarity in names is interesting, but I have been unable to determine whether the Calhoun Cravens were relatives of the Paragould clan.

A farm near Paragould, AR (not the Craven property) showing forest

Gail Craven Fail

Five years after the Cravens settled in Greene County, Arkansas seceded from the union. Andrew Robert was in his mid fifties at the time. I have not found any records indicating that he fought in the Civil War. I am not even sure which side Andrew favored in the war. There were few slaves in his part of the state, but there were lots of pro-slavery white folks, and plenty of racism. I imagine that he favored the Confederates.

The area around Paragould includes several famous Civil War Union troop movement routes, including the routes taken by soldiers going to fight at Little Rock and Pea Ridge. The town of Paragould (incorporated after Andrew Robert's death) is somewhat infamous as a white-only "sundown town." The few African Americans in the area were frequently harassed and threatened by the KKK during reconstruction. There were no schools for black children in Paragould until 1948. Even today, the black population of Paragould is less than one percent.

Gorman Craven, my own father, prided himself on being unbigoted in his behavior, but he was actually very racist. He believed that white people were genetically superior because of having larger brains. His thinking was based on the work of an American biologist and anatomist, Samuel Morton, who published his crackpot ideas in the 1840s. Many people used his work as a justification for slavery. He claimed to have measured the brain capacity of many different kinds of people. He said that African people had smaller brains and were therefore less intelligent than whites. Gorman read about Morton's ideas almost a century later, in the 1930s. But I believe the family racism was already well ingrained when Gorman read about Morton's work. In the late 1970s I gave him a copy of Gould's book, *The Mismeasure of Man*, which explained how Morton's measurements and data were flawed. I am not sure that reading this book changed his mind. It is interesting that only a few generations before, my father's Quaker ancestors preached against slavery.

Andrew's son William Jasper (1845-1883) was sixteen years old when the Civil War began, and twenty when it ended. I don't know whether he fought in the war. His first child was born two years after the war ended, so it is reasonable that he spent some time in the Confederate Army. Ancestry.com shows that almost 500 men named William Craven were listed as soldiers in that war! Some of these must have been repetitions. I did not find a William Jasper or William J. Craven on the Arkansas rolls.

William Jasper followed Craven family tradition by farming. His wife was a Tennessee woman, Sarah Trentham, who outlived him by twenty years. William lived to be only 38 years old, but in his relatively short life had ten children with Sarah. They first farmed in Greene County, AK, then moved to White County, southeast of his parents' home.

Farmland in White County, AR

After William Jasper died, Sarah married an older man with eight children, who had outlived three wives before her. She had one child with him. Merging the two large families, with 18 children, must have been an interesting experience. But I imagine that Sarah had little choice. A woman alone could not have handled the work involved in farming when she had the responsibility for so many children.

William Jasper's oldest son, William Andrew Craven (1866-1931) was my great grandfather. At age nineteen (about three years after his father died), he married seventeen-year old Malinda Combs. I am not sure how much education William got, but probably not a lot. His wife Malinda finished 7th grade, which was typical for farm kids of that period. They had nine children, and continued the family pattern of moving. In 1900, William and Malinda were in White County, Arkansas. Ten years later, they were living in Atoka County, Oklahoma, an area once occupied by Choctaw Indians. While in Oklahoma, William's son Marion Andrew (my grandfather) met and married his wife Stella.

Rural Atoka County, OK

William Andrew died at age 65, in Corpus Christi, Texas. At the time of his death, he was the proprietor of a small grocery store. He was also a Baptist preacher.

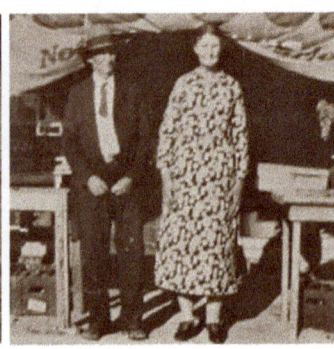

William Andrew and Malinda Craven

William Andrew died at sixty-five, but Malinda lived to be ninety-one years old. She was bed-bound at the end of her life due to a broken hip, probably something that could be repaired with modern medicine. My father's aunt Lillian helped to care for her, as did my grandmother, Stella. Malinda became almost completely blind after the broken hip. I met her a few times when I was in grade school, and we exchanged letters. I was impressed by her sweet nature and the tolerance she showed for what must have been very difficult disabilities. When she wrote to me, Grandma Stella helped hold the paper, so she would not write one line over another. In spite of her blindness, her writing was legible. She died when I was eleven.

By the early 1900s, when William Andrew and Malinda moved to southeastern Oklahoma, the American agricultural frontier was almost over. Farmland was no longer cheaply available for purchase or rent in the more eastern states. White people began taking over what had been Indian Territory in the mid-west, and by about 1900 most of the tenant farmers in Oklahoma were white.

William Andrew and Malinda's youngest and oldest child were 27 years apart. This meant that some of their grandchildren were close in age to their children, just as in Peter Craven's family. My father Gorman grew up knowing uncles and aunts that were not too much older than he, and therefore more like siblings.

Three were particularly close to him: Uncle Alvin, who was 12 years older, Aunt Lillian, 9 years older and Uncle Roy, 6 years older.

Alvin married Blanche Reeves. He died in 1963, but Blanche lived to be 91 years old, dying in 2000. They had several children.

Alvin and Blanche

Lillian was a nurse. She married Isaac Floyd (Jack) Gidden. She died in 1966. Her birth name was Lillian Adeline Lee Craven, but she called herself Lillian Lee Craven.

Lillian at graduation from nursing school

Lillian caring for Malinda

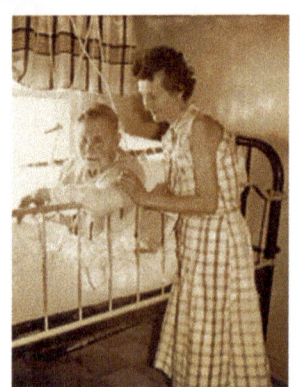

Roy married Gladys Sweeten. He died of a heart attack in 1960 at age 52, and she lived until age 74, dying in 1986.

Roy and Gladys had a son, Leslie Leroy, who died at age 30, only six months after his father. Leroy had osteomyelitis in one leg as a teenager and was confined to bed. He was cured when penicillin became available, and went on to play high school football and later, was a paratrooper. Leroy had a strong resemblance to my father.

Leslie Leroy

Loymay was only 2 years older than Papa, but he never mentioned her to me. In fact, I had never heard of her until I began researching family history. She married in 1931, at age 19, but I don't know to whom. The marriage was recorded in a family Bible, and was reported to me by Peggy Wilson. Family stories say that Loymay was very pretty, and she went to California hoping to make a career in movies. She became a gangster's girlfriend, and just disappeared one day in California. The family thought she was murdered by her criminal boyfriend or by one of his rivals.

Marion Andrew Craven, my grandfather, was William Andrew's fourth child. The same year Loymay was born (1912), Marion married Stella Myrtle Wyrick. He was twenty-one; she was seventeen. For the first few years of their marriage, they lived with her parents, Bud and Millie Wyrick, and Marion worked on the Wyrick farm in Oklahoma. Marion and Stella had three boys, Gorman Andrew (my father), Truett Wyrick, and Marvin Elvis, over five years. The two oldest boys' first names came from Baptist preachers. But Marion and Stella kept Andrew, a traditional Craven name, as a middle name for the oldest, and the second son's middle name was Stella's maiden name. I am not sure where Marvin's names came from.

I was allowed to call Stella "Grandma," because by the time I came along, she had reconciled herself to being a grandmother. When my sister Sue (the first grandchild) was born, Stella was only forty-one and thought she was too young to be a grandmother. My older siblings were instructed to called Marion "Daddy Andy," and his wife was "Mama Stella." Daddy Andy died when I was five, and my only memory of him is that he was a very tall skinny man. My brothers (Carl and Jerry Craven) have both published books with stories of Daddy Andy.

Census data says that Marion completed 8th grade, and Stella finished 6th grade. They were both very religious. He was a Baptist preacher, as was his father. Daddy Andy moved his family a lot. One of the reasons for that was his penchant for seducing young women. Sometimes the family had to move very quickly when an irate father or husband caught him with a woman. His hypocritical behavior is a very interesting contradiction. I think he must have been tormented with guilt.

Marion worked as a laborer, carpenter, farmer, and anything else he could manage. He was apparently an intelligent and charming man. Papa told me he was also somewhat lazy, but this might have been due to poor health. He had a tendency toward anemia, and had heart disease.

Grandma Stella visited me when I was a married adult. She was interested in my birth control pills and said that I should be grateful to have them. Grandma also said that after her third child she told Daddy Andy there would be no more sex, and that they would have to live as brother and sister. They had married in 1912. After 1917, when their third son came along, they were never again sexually intimate. This may help explain, though not excuse, Daddy Andy's adultery.

In 1920, when their children were still little, Marion and Stella lived with her parents in Oklahoma. By 1928 they had left the Wyrick farm and were settled in the Rio Grande River Valley near the very small town of Presidio, Texas. My father Gorman, the oldest, was fourteen. Carl says that Marion picked Presidio because he could probably find farm work there. The climate was mild, with a long growing season. They were migrant workers, living much of the time in a tent. It was a kind of gypsy existence. Mama often said that the reason Papa never cared much about what his house looked like is that he considered anything better than a tent.

They moved around as needed, following the work. Within a couple of years the family moved five hundred miles east, to Refugio, Texas, just north of Corpus Christi, where Marion's brother Alvin was living. By 1940, the two oldest boys were married and Marion and his wife were farming in Benton County Arkansas, near the town of Pea Ridge.

I believe it was when they were living in a

farmhouse near Corpus Christi that Grandma Stella got rid of her wood-burning stove. She wanted a gas stove. Certainly she must have become very tired of cooking on outdoor fires or tricky wood stoves. She asked Daddy Andy several times for a gas stove, but he always refused. Finally, she hauled her wood stove out into the yard. When Daddy Andy got home, she was attempting to break it apart with an ax. She told him that she would simply not cook another meal on it. He bought a gas stove.

During the period in the late 1920s when the Cravens were migrant farm workers, one of my father's jobs was to bring home game, mostly rabbits, for the cook pot. He got a .22 caliber long rifle pistol for his fourteenth birthday and became an excellent shot. One day when he was out hunting, a rattlesnake bit him in his right hand. He had been squatting for a "call of nature" and reached behind him for a clump of grass to wipe with. Instead of grass, he grabbed a rattler. He made it to the local veterinarian, who injected him with anti-venom and got him to a hospital. In a couple of days, the hand was so swollen that a physician recommended amputation. Papa refused, and his father backed him up, saying that it was Gorman's decision. He recovered, but he had some severe arthritis in that hand when he was in his fifties, and blamed that on the snakebite.

Papa left high school in 10th grade, to help support his family. This was at the beginning of the Great Depression. When he met my mother, Bell Carlson, he was working on the docks in Corpus Christi as a longshoreman, loading and unloading ships. In 1935, when he was twenty-one and she was eighteen, they married. He decided that he should learn a trade. Or maybe Mama decided that for him. In any event, it was a good move, since after WWII jobs for longshoremen were drastically reduced due to mechanization.

I think some of Papa's appeal for Mama (besides being good looking, smart and muscular) was that the Craven family always had food in the house. Mama came from a middle class white-collar family that was not at all prepared for the Great Depression. Her father Oscar lost his bank job in 1929, and their house in Austin was repossessed. He was able to get an accounting job in Corpus Christi, but not long after the move his wife Ella died. Between the Great Depression and his own personal loss, Oscar fell into the bottle. He was employed most of the time but he made little money, drank a lot, and Mama's home life was stressful. The depression was a great shock to her. She had lived a comfortable life in Austin, in a well-built house with nice furniture, a full pantry, and beautiful clothing. Then, in a couple of years, she lost all that and her mother. Oscar moved them to a Mexican barrio, and they lived in a house with no plumbing and a dirt floor.

The Cravens were poorly educated but very smart people, and they managed poverty more gracefully due to generations of experience. They grew much of their own food, hunted, fished, saved scraps of everything, and knew how to can, dry and otherwise preserve food. These backcountry skills allowed them to survive the Great Depression better than many other people. In addition, Marion and his sons were particularly clever at rebuilding and repairing machinery.

Within four years of his marriage Papa was a licensed plumber. They had three children in the first six years of their marriage: Carolyn Susan, Carl Andrew, and Gerald Allen. Eight years after Jerry was born, they had me.

1939, Bell (age 21) with Malinda Craven. Children are Carl, Roy's son Leroy, and Sue.

Like his father, Papa moved his family a lot. He followed the work, and seemed not to care much about the effects on his children. Of course, his parents had moved a lot, too, so it seemed normal to him. Sue attended thirteen different schools by the time she was in third grade. It says a lot that as an adult Sue settled in west Texas and never left. She has lived on the same street in Big Spring for almost fifty years.

In the fall of 1941 they were living in Corpus Christi. Papa's uncles were working in Fort Smith, Arkansas and had written that there was plenty of work. So my parents sold their furniture. They got rid of everything they considered non-essential, including all of the kid's toys and Sue's beloved Raggedy Ann doll. Jerry was an infant, but the other two kids were old enough to feel upset by the loss of their belongings.

Papa built a trailer and loaded it with their remaining bare minimum household items (including Mama's gas-powered washing machine). My parents filled the backseat of their old Ford with pillows and blankets to make a flat area for the kids to roll around. They drove to his parent's place in Benton County, near Pea Ridge, Arkansas, where they were share cropping. Uncle Truett, his wife Cleo, their baby Mary and uncle Marvin were all living with Marion and Stella. After Papa's group arrived it must have been a fairly crowded house. The kids and Mama stayed on the farm until Papa got a job, then they moved to Fort Smith (about 80 miles away) and rented a furnished apartment.

Areas near Pea Ridge, AR

Before he moved his family to Fort Smith Papa visited the local tire dealers and bought all the used tires he could get, storing them on the farm. Some were almost worn-out, and he was able to get them free. He figured that with war right around the corner, there might be a shortage of tires. He was right.

During the war, he always had tires for his own car, and was able to sell the rest for a small profit. His forethought paid off, since the Japanese attacked Pearl Harbor in December of 1941, and America was at war.

Sue was five years old when the family moved to Arkansas. She remembers the huge pile of tires our father collected. She also remembers that the barn caught fire one night while the family was staying with Daddy Andy and Grandma Stella. Marvin wanted to run into the barn and save some tools, but Daddy Andy was afraid he would get burned. So he told Marvin that his job was to watch out for Sue. None of the kids was allowed to go to sleep in the house, because the house itself might have caught fire, too, and then they would be trapped. They waited outside. Sue got cold, and Marvin gave her his long-sleeved shirt to wear. It smelled bad, but she did not complain. Even at age five she had been taught good manners and that complaining about things was a waste of time.

Papa got a job as a plumber in Fort Smith in January of 1942. He worked there for a while and then moved again, following the construction work. He made so much money working in Fort Smith that he was able to buy a 40-acre farm near Pea Ridge, complete with brooder houses and a five-room house. His parents moved onto that farm and stayed there for several years, raising chickens. Marion also preached at a local Baptist church. Papa added a bathroom and a kitchen sink to the house, and a pump to bring water from the well. There was some consternation about the bathroom, as his parents thought having a toilet inside the house was not sanitary. But Sue liked having a bathroom because the outhouse was full of huge spiders.

Sue remembers that the farmhouse had five or six layers of wallpaper. The bottom layer was Civil War era newspaper, put up to stop the wind blowing through. Grandma Stella repapered, and when she stripped off the old wallpaper she got arsenic poisoning. Fortunately the family doctor was able to diagnose her condition and she recovered. In the 1800s, many kinds of wallpaper were made with arsenic-based dyes or were glued with arsenic paste. The poison prevented roaches or mice from nibbling the paper. Mild arsenic poisoning causes vomiting and diarrhea, but heavy exposures lead to much nastier symptoms, or even death.

The house had no insulation (other than wallpaper) and was very cold in the winter. Once, when Papa brought his family to visit, the three kids were all put into one bed, with several hot water bottles for warmth. During the night, some of those water bottles were kicked onto the floor, and in the morning they were filled with slush ice. Mama was not happy about visiting in the winter.

During the war, gasoline was rationed. After the work played out in Fort Smith and the family had moved to southeast Texas, Papa rigged up the car to run on kerosene, which was not rationed. It would have to be started with gasoline, but then he could switch to kerosene and keep it going. Sue remembers the click sound of the switch, and the change in smell as the car switched back and forth between the two fuel tanks.

The kerosene-powered car came in handy when

the next-door neighbors' dog became rabid. Both the father and the little boy had to undergo the Pasteur vaccine, which was the only prevention for rabies at the time. It involved a series of injections into abdominal fat, over a period of several days. Mama drove them to Galveston for their treatment, and took all three of her kids along. They were able to manage the trips because the car ran on kerosene.

Papa's heart condition prevented him from fighting in WW II, but he was pretty constantly employed during the war years. In 1946, the year after the war ended, he got a job in Venezuela. The family spent several years there, had me, and returned to Texas when I was three years old. Our young Texas cousins were wondering whether I would be a brown baby since I was born in South America, where most people are brown. But I turned out to be fair skinned and blonde like the rest of Mama's kids.

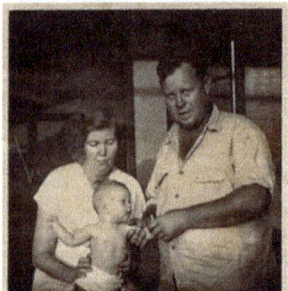
Bell, Baby Gail and Gorman, 1949

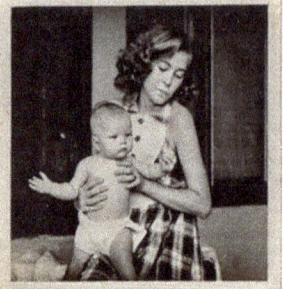
Baby Gail and Sue, 1949

Daddy Andy was upset about Papa's move to Venezuela. Many years later, when Jerry was considering moving to Malaysia for a year or two, Papa told him to go, and that he would never stand in the way of his children's desire to live in another country and have an adventure.

In South America, I learned to speak Spanish as well as English, and somehow decided that the Spanish term "Papa" was what I would call our father. The other kids all called him "Daddy" or "Dad."

After we returned to Texas, Papa got a plumbing job in Port Arthur, and our parents bought a big, ramshackle house prone to electrical fires. Mama's father, Oscar Carlson, lived with us. Mama worked as a telephone operator. Sue stayed in Corpus to attend community college for a couple of years and then she moved to Port Arthur, and attended Lamar Tech in Beaumont for her English degree. Carl and Jerry also got degrees at Lamar, and each of the oldest three kids married and moved out. For a while Papa ran his own plumbing business, until he was forced into bankruptcy after a shopping center contract folded and left him with a huge load of debt.

While we were in Venezuela, Daddy Andy and Stella left the farm that papa had bought for them. Apparently Andy got someone pregnant, and was "read out" of the Baptist church. This means that he was found guilty of immorality by the church members, and publicly condemned. The social ostracism was too much to bear. So they packed up and moved to the Texas panhandle. Within about a year, they had to leave that area too, for the same reason. This time they moved to Friendswood, a Quaker community near Houston. Apparently Daddy Andy left the women alone after that. When they left Friendswood, it was for a job north of San Antonio, managing an angora goat farm. While working that job, Daddy Andy died of a heart attack. He was sixty-three. I was five years old, and my family had been back in the United States for two years. I know we went to his funeral, but I don't remember any of it.

After Daddy Andy died, Grandma Stella moved back to Pea Ridge. This time she lived on a farm owned by a friend (Lena) who was widowed. The two women raised chickens, grew a huge vegetable garden, and made beautiful quilts. While I was growing up, we made many trips to see Stella, and she sometimes came to Port Arthur for extended visits. I have many happy memories of visiting her farm. Before Lena tore down the old farmhouse and built a new two-bedroom home with insulation, she and Stella managed with little indoor plumbing. There was a tap in the kitchen, but no hot water heater. The house was heated only by a couple of fireplaces. Once, when we visited in the wintertime, Grandma spilled some water on the dining room floor. It immediately froze solid. We found her in the morning, ironing the floor. She had laid an old towel over the spill, and the iron melted the ice enough so the water was absorbed. I thought it was an ingenious way of removing ice from the floor. It was also a lesson in the importance of insulation.

When Stella got too old to work, she lived with Truett and Cleo. She is buried in Pea Ridge, Arkansas. Stella had family roots in Pea Ridge, which may be why she tended to gravitate back toward that part of the country. Her mother Millie Wyrick was born and died there. Her father Bud Wyrick fought in the Civil War Battle of Pea Ridge.

In 1969, after I had married and my grandfather died, my parents moved to a smaller nearby town. The big house burned down after they left. Its electrical system was old in the 1950s, and no doubt it was an old wire that caused the final fire. In 1972, my parents divorced. It was the best thing they could have done. Their marriage had been shaky for years. Both remarried and were much happier. They had stayed together because of the mutual responsibility of caring for their children and Mama's father.

Papa's second wife was Evelyn Dykes, the widow of a long-time friend. She was a more subservient woman, who did pretty much what Papa asked. This was completely different from Mama's behavior, and seemed to suit him better. He mellowed out after marrying Evelyn, and even did housework (although not much) and would go shopping for groceries. I was amazed.

Papa retired when he was forced into it. He had never intended to live long enough for retirement. For years, he had been lying about his age to the Union Hall. Evelyn dyed his white hair brown, and he passed himself off as a younger man. In spite of his heart condition, diabetes, several heart attacks and kidney stones, he was in pretty good physical shape after his divorce. He found regular work as a plumber or pipe-fitter at one of the many Southeast Texas oil refineries.

But in the early 1980s, he began having kidney pain. He was diagnosed with kidney cancer and one kidney was removed. The oncologist who treated him said that the kidney cancer was probably caused by lead exposure, from many years of handling lead solder. The cancer had already spread into his pelvic bones, so he had radiation treatment. This kept him going a bit longer, but he was in a fair amount of bone pain and dreaded the possibility of a long, drawn-out death in a hospital. He and Evelyn moved to central

Texas, near Leander, where they lived in a mobile home bought for them by Evelyn's children. One morning they woke up, and Evelyn went into the kitchen to make tea. During the few minutes she was gone, he fell over dead from a heart attack, sparing him the dreaded hospital death. Evelyn followed him in a few years. They are both buried in Leander.

Two weeks before he died, Papa converted to Evelyn's brand of Christianity. He told me he planned to do this, in order to save her from worry about where he might go after death. But he did not intend to do it too soon, because he really did not want to attend too many Sunday church meetings. It was the last kindness he could do for her. She believed that only members of her particular church went to heaven.

Mama married Glenn Meek, the widower of an old friend. Glenn and his wife Ruth were college students with my sister Sue at community college in Corpus Christi. Glenn had been in the Navy for over twenty years. He and his wife went back to college after he retired from the Navy, and eventually both became high school teachers. The Meeks were surrogate parents, and often fed Sue home cooked meals.

Glenn and Ruth settled near Port Arthur as high school teachers, and the two families were able to visit. After Mama was divorced and Ruth died, Glenn and Mama began seeing each other. They eventually married and moved to Big Spring Texas, where they lived happily in one of Sue's rent houses until Glenn died. Mama outlived him by several years, but had several small strokes that left her periodically confused. It was probably a stroke that killed her. She died peacefully while napping, with her cat in her arms.

Just before her death, she mailed cash to each of her children except Carl. After Mama's funeral, Sue found an envelope with Carl's name on it, but no address. Inside was the same amount of cash she had sent to the rest of us. Apparently she could not remember or locate Carl's address. Sue addressed the envelope and mailed it off, thinking that was what Mama had intended, and believing that Mama gave away her money because she knew death was near.

My uncle Truett Craven married Mapie Cleo Cooke and had three children: Mary Carolyn, Truett Andrew (Andy) and Stella Florence, all still living at the time I am writing (2014). When I was a child, I always thought Aunt Cleo's real name was "Cleopatra," which I thought was very classy and romantic. I was disappointed to discover that her name was just Cleo. Nobody ever used her first name, Mapie.

Uncle Truett and aunt Cleo came to see us often when I was a child, and I stayed with them a few times. I liked Truett, who looked a lot like Papa. His hands had the same shape and battered appearance as my father's. He was an excellent carpenter. Truett was always nice to me, but as an adult I found out that he was abusive to his own children. Cleo was a warm and affectionate woman. I remember being comforted by her when a green tree snake fell down my blouse while I was visiting her house. After she saw I was unhurt, she hugged and patted me till I calmed down.

Marvin married Doreen Olivia Lawrence and had one child, Sandra Ann Craven, (1943-1999) who was a nurse. I don't remember ever meeting either Doreen or Sandra. Marvin was the family black sheep: a drinker, drug user, womanizer, and thief. My parents told me that his wife Doreen was a heroin addict, and Marvin stole to keep both of them supplied with drugs. Papa excused his behavior by telling us that Marvin had been kicked in the head by a horse when he was young.

Marvin divorced Doreen (not sure when) and in 1976 married his cousin Velma Sustaire. Mama told me that Marvin had always loved Velma, but they were forbidden to marry because they were first cousins. Velma's mother Ethel was Daddy Andy's sister. Marvin and Velma found each other again after they were older. Apparently they were happy together.

I have not written about my generation or our children and grandchildren. That will be up to a later descendant, one who can tell all the scandalous stories of our lives.

Some of the sources used, not in any particular order:

1. Website for the Church of St. Peter and St.Paul, in Bolton-by-Bowland. List of rectors, starting in 1304.

2. Genealogical survey of British peers, at thepeerage.com

3. http://www.domesdaybook.co.uk/faqs.html#1

4. The Knights of England, Published 1906, Printed and published for the Central chancery of the orders of knighthood, Sherratt and Hughes in London.

5. http://genforum.genealogy.com/craven/messages/1368.html About Sir Anthony Craven

6. http://facstaff.bloomu.edu/mhickey/High%20Middle%20Ages%20religious_and_intellectual_life.htm About the Middle Ages

7. http://www.redwulf.info/rural/index.html Medieval rural life

8. The Project Gutenberg EBook of Parish Priests and Their People in the Middle Ages in England, by Edward L. Cutts, published 1898, released digitally 2013.

9. http://www.sarumcustomary.org.uk/context/medievalchurch/churches.php Worship in the Medieval Cathedral and Parish Church

10. http://randolphhistory.wordpress.com/tag/revolutionary-war/ Notes on the History of Randolph County, NC

11. http://files.usgwarchives.net/nc/orange/military/revwar/regulatr.txt About the Regulators

12. Centennial History of Alamance County 1849 1949, by Walter Whitaker. Printed in the United States by the Dowd Press, Inc. Charlotte, NC. Online

at rootsweb.com

13. http://www.longprestonheritage.org.uk/shop/Review%20by%20Bill%20Mitchell.pdf Landscapes and Townscapes of North Craven, by W.R.Mitchell, MBE.

14. http://www.fantompowa.net/Flame/slavery_in_london.html cites William Craven's investment in slavery

15. Turning Points in Baptist History: A Festschrift in Honor of Harry Leon McBeth, Michael Edward Williams , Walter B. Shurden , Mercer University Press, 2008.

16. http://wesley.nnu.edu/holiness-classics-library/history-of-the-methodist-episcopal-church/volume-1-book-i-chapter-3/

17. Arkansas: Civil War Through Reconstruction, online Encyclopedia of Arkansas.

18. The Norman People and Their Existing Descendants in the British Dominions and the United States of America, 1874, Henry King, Google eBook

19. http://www.genuki.org.uk/big/eng/YKS/index.html#Towns Yorkshire history

20. http://www.westjerseyhistory.org/books/njaV21/njaSalemDeedsLiberB.shtml copy of Anne Craven's land purchase

21. Documents Relating to the Colonial History of the State of New Jersey, published by the NJ Historical Society, 1939.

22. http://www.findagrave.com/cgi-bin/fg.cgi?page=vcsr&GSvcid=193942 Craven line memorials.

23. The Roots of Appalachian Christianity: The Life and Legacy of Elder Shubal, By Elder John Sparks, 2001, Google ebooks

24. http://www.earlyamerica.com/review/2009_summer_fall/regulators-movement.html The Regulators Movement in The Carolina, by Nathan C. Traylor

25. http://digital.ncdcr.gov/cdm/ref/collection/p15012coll1/id/8060 Eli Asbury and Margaret Ann England Craven Family Bible Records.

26. The Yorkshire Archaeological Journal, Volume 13, 1895, article regarding the Appletreewick Cravens.

27. http://hoydensandfirebrands.blogspot.com/2011/09/yorkshire-dick-whittington-sir-william.html The Yorkshire "Dick Whittington" Sir William Craven and the rise of the Craven Dynasty, a blog about the use of Craven's love for the Queen of Bohemia in love stories.

28. http://connection.ebscohost.com/c/letters/70394526/right-honourable-william-lord-graven-baron-hamfted-marfham A letter from English poet John Donne to the Right Honourable William Lord Craven, Baron of Hamsted-Marsham, regarding Donne's asking of permission from Lord Craven to print the poems.

29. The Journal of George Fox, 1911, Google ebook.

30. The Battle Abbey Roll with an Account of Some Normal Lineages, by the Duchess of Cleveland, 1889, Google ebook

31. Descendants of Peter Craven, Randolph County North Carolina, by Mary Craven Purvis, 1985, Hunsucker Printing Co., Asheboro, NC

32. 280 Years with the Peter Craven Family 1712-1993, Randolph County, NC, by Mary Craven

Purvis, self-published.

33. Adventures from the Last Century, by Carl Craven, 2012, Angelina River Press.

34. Saving a Songbird and Other True Stories from Venezuela to Texas, by Jerry Craven, 2012, Slough Press.

35. Coyotes Ate my Cat, Memoirs of a Biologist, by Gail Fail, 2013, Angelina River Press.

Gail Craven Fail

Craven ancestors

* indicates a Craven in my direct line

Sir John Craven	
born	1485 Appletreewick, Craven, Yorkshire, England
died	1585, age 100
profession	Farmer, knight
married	1507 Miss Simpson, 1491-1516
Children one	*William

Sir William Craven	
born	1506 Appletreewick
died	1596 London, age 90
profession	Farmer, knight
married	1539 Beatrix Hunter, 1513- 1598
Children three	*Anthony 1541-1636 Henry 1543-1603 William 1545-1618

Sir Anthony (Anthonie) Craven	
born	1541 Burnsall, Yorkshire
died	1636 Bath, England, age 95
profession	Knight
married	1576 Anne Crofte, 1564-1612
Children six	Jane 1577 Marye 1578 Isabell 1581 John 1584 *Thomas 1585 William 1596

Craven Family History

Sir Thomas Craven (s)	
born	1585 England
died	1636, age 51
profession	Knight
married	1624 Margaret Craven b 1603.
Children six	Richard b. 1624
	Sir Anthony, b 1626
	John 1629
	*Sir Robert 1632-1672
	Mary Clerke 1634-1707
	Sir William 1636

Sir Robert Craven (s)	
born	1632 Stepney, Middlesex, England
died	1672 England, Age 40
profession	Knight
married	Ann Croft (Ann of Lyme House, Middlesex, England) b 1625 England, d 1681, NJ, age 56 at death
Children Three or four	Thomas 1668- 1730
	Ann Craven 1670-1754, m Isaac Warner
	*Peter 1671-1745
	maybe another son

(Joshua) Peter Craven	also called Peter Craven, or Peter Craven I
born	1671, Stepney Parish, Shadwell, Middlesex, England
died	1745 North Carolina, 74 yrs old
profession	Husbandman (was given land from his mother)
married	1698 Mary Holland, b 1670, d 1726 Va
Children Three or four	Richard b 1710
	*Peter 1712-1791
	maybe a third son
	maybe a daughter Rachel, m Abraham Crow

Gail Craven Fail

Peter Craven	Also called Peter the Patriarch, Potter, Regulator
born	1712 Penn Area, Salem County, NJ
died	1794 Randolph County N.C, buried in Coleridge, Craven Cemetery, 82 yrs old
profession	Potter, farmer
married	unknown
Children Seven. Additional info on sons is from a Craven Family Bible, digitized in North Carolina Digital Collections	*Thomas 1742-1817 (two sons were preachers) Peter 1744-1840 (one son was a preacher) Joseph 1746-abt 1840 (grandson founded Trinity College) John 1750-52? -1833 (two sons were Baptist preachers) Daniel 1759-1846 (Primitive Baptist preacher) Henry 1762-1843 (held for the King in the Revolutionary War) Sarah? Rebecca?

Below I added the number of children born to each of Thomas' sons. This is an indication of the sheer number of Craven relatives we have, from just six generations back.

Thomas Craven	
born	1742, Augusta County VA
died	1817 Randolph County N.C. 76 yrs old
profession	Potter, farmer, Justice of the Peace
married	1761-63? Frances 1746-1801
Children 12, and at least 56 grandchildren	Peter b. 1766 -1849, farmer, preacher, 8 children *John b. 1770 -1832, minister, 13 children Mary Hannah b. 1772, m Henry Bray Sarah b. 1774 -1817, one son Thomas b. 1775 -1857 potter, 11 children Samuel b. 1777, 14 children Jacob b. 1779, 9 children Catherine b. 1782 no info Solomon 1785-1833 potter, farmer, Justice of the Peace Frances b: 1788 no info 2 more daughters, Jenny and Mary no dates

Craven Family History

John Craven	
born	1770, N. C.
died	1832, 62 yrs old
profession	Potter and Methodist minister.
married	Mary Vandervere or Vanderford 1790 or 1791 (b 1772) Second wife Susannah McMasters (b ca. 1778)
Children 13	Elizabeth Craven 1793- Thomas W Craven 1794-1880 John V. Craven 1798- 1877 Arminta (Minty) Craven 1799- 1875 Anderson Craven 1801- 1872, potter and minister * Andrew Robert Craven, 1802-1867, potter Isaac Newton Craven 1805-1881 potter Mary (Polly) Craven 1806-1850 Peter Craven 1807-1830 Enoch Spinks Craven b 1810-1893, potter Andrew Jackson Craven 1815-1899 Nancy Olive Craven 1818- Eliza Craven b 1821-1892

Gail Craven Fail

Andrew Robert Craven (s)	
born	1802 or 1803, Randolph County, N.C.
died	1867, Paragould, Greene County, AR buried in Center Hill Cemetery, Paragould 65 yrs old
profession	Farmer, potter
Married	circa 1825 to Elizabeth Garner or Gardner 1804-1845
	1845 Nancy Ann Spencer (or Smith) 1827-1880
Children 15-16. Looks like the wives each had a baby every 2 years or so. Sarah and James are born in the same year. Maybe one was miscarried? Or were they twins?	Hannah 1829
	Carole Lavinia 1831
	John Wesley Craven 1834
	Eliza 1836-1900
	Samira Susan 1838
	Sarah 1842
	James A Craven 1842-1883
	William James 1844
	*William Jasper 1845-1883
	In 1845, Elizabeth died. In 1846 he married Nancy. With second wife he had:
	George Washington Craven 1847
	And about 6 more, last one born 1868

William Jasper Craven	
born	1845, Tippah County, Mississippi
died	1883, White County, AR 38 yrs old.
Profession	farmer
married	Sarah Isabelle Trentham, b 1845or 1846 Tennessee, d 1903, White County, AR
Children nine	*William A Craven 1867-1931
	Mary Jane Craven 1869-1958
	James N Craven 1871-1902
	Joel Craven 1873-
	Malinda A. Craven 1875-1880
	John T Craven 1876-1880
	Luther Cornelius Craven 1878-1951
	Gertie A Craven 1881
	Clara J Craven 1882

Craven Family History

William Andrew Craven	
born	1866, White County Arkansas
died	1931, Corpus Christi, TX, buried in White Hill Memorial Park, 65 yrs old
profession	Farmer, preacher
Married	1885 Malinda (Melinda) Combs, b 1869 Indiana, d 1960, buried in Henryetta, OK, age 91.
Children nine	Claude 1885-1886 Amy S (also called Annie) 1887-1964 Ily 1889-1890 *Marion Andrew 1891-1954 Ethel 1896-1960 William Alvin 1902-1963 Roy Carroll 1908-1960 Lillian Adeline 1905-1966 m Isaac Floyd (Jack) Gidden Loymay, 1912. Death date unknown

Marion Andrew Craven (Daddy Andy)	
born	March 18, 1891
died	July 28, 1954, Boerne TX 63 yrs old. Buried in Boerne Cemetery, Boerne Texas, Kendall County.
profession	Carpenter, preacher, farmer
married	1912 Stella Myrtle Wyrick, b 1895 OK, d 1984, Benton Arkansas, buried Pea Ridge.
Children three	*Gorman Andrew Craven 1914-1986, age 72. Truett Wyrick Craven, 1915-1983 age 68. Marvin Elvis Craven 1917-1993, age 75.

Gorman Andrew Craven	
born	1914 Overbrook, Love County, OK
died	d 1986, TX 72 yrs old, in Leander, Williamson County, TX
profession	plumber/pipefitter
married	1935, Charlotte Rosebell Carlson, 1918 - 2005, Divorced 1972, she remarried to Glenn Meek. Gorman remarried Evelyn Dykes in 1972.
Children	Carolyn Susan King, 1936- Carl Andrew Craven, 1938- Gerald Allen Craven, 1941- Gail Laverne Craven, 1949-

Truett Wyrick Craven	
Born	1915
Died	1983, age 68, Meridian TX, buried in Morgan Cemetery, Bosque, TX
Profession	Carpenter
married	Mapie Cleo Cooke b 1923
children	Mary Carolyn Craven 1940- Truett Andrew 1941- Stella Florence Craven 1945-

Marvin Elvis Craven	
Born	1917
Died	1993, age 75
Profession	Carpenter
Married	Doreen Olivia Lawrence and Velma R. Sustaire
children	Sandra Ann Craven 1943-1999

Notes

Notes

Notes

Notes

Notes

www.ingramcontent.com/pod-product-compliance
Lightning Source LLC
Chambersburg PA
CBHW050817090426
42736CB00022B/3483